A Special Gift

PRESENTED TO:

....

FROM:

....

DATE:

....

A Christmas Greeting:

....

....

....

....

....

....

....

....

THE GLORY
_of_
CHRISTMAS

CHARLES SWINDOLL

MAX LUCADO

COUNTRYMAN

Copyright © 1999 by J. Countryman
Published by J. Countryman, a division of Thomas Nelson, Inc., Nashville, TN 37214

Compiled and edited by Terri Gibbs

Photographic Acknowledgments:
Bill Brooks/Masterfile, pages 41, 77, 120.
Ron Stroud/Masterfile, pages 19, 56, 61, 85, 94, 101, 119, 125.
Janet Foster/Masterfile, pages 7, 28, 82.
David Muir/Masterfile, pages 36, 46, 69.
Daryl Benson/Masterfile, pages 8, 15, 42, 52, 65, 102, 108, 113, 129, 140.
Jim Craigmyle/Masterfile, pages 3, 25, 89, 134.

Designed by Koechel Peterson & Associates, Inc.
Minneapolis, Minnesota.

ISBN: 0-8499-5561-0

Printed in China

THE GLORY *of* CHRISTMAS

hristmas comes each year to draw people in from the cold.

Like tiny frightened sparrows, shivering in the winter cold, many live their lives on the barren branches of heartbreak, disappointment, and loneliness, lost in thoughts of shame, self-pity, guilt, or failure. One blustery day follows another, and the only company they keep is with fellow-strugglers who land on the same branches, confused and unprotected.

(CONTINUED)

We try so hard to attract them into the warmth. Week after week church bells ring. Choirs sing. Preachers preach. Lighted churches send out their beacon. But nothing seems to bring in those who need warmth the most.

Then, as the year draws to a close, Christmas offers its wonderful message. Emmanuel. God with us. He who resided in Heaven, co-equal and co-eternal with the Father and the Spirit, willingly descended into our world. He breathed our air, felt our pain, knew our sorrows, and died for our sins. He didn't come to frighten us, but to show us the way to warmth and safety.

CHARLES SWINDOLL
THE FINISHING TOUCH

The gift is not

from man to God.

It is from

God to man.

Max Lucado

he conclusion is unavoidable: self-salvation simply does not work. Man has no way to save himself.

But Paul announces that God has a way. Where man fails God excels. Salvation comes from heaven downward, not earth upward. "A new day from heaven will dawn upon us" (Luke 1:78). "Every good action and every perfect gift is from God" (James 1:17).

Please note: Salvation is God-given, God-driven, God-empowered, and God-originated. The gift is not from man to God. It is from God to man.

(CONTINUED)

Grace is created by God and given to man. . . . On the basis of this point alone, Christianity is set apart from any other religion in the world. . . . Every other approach to God is a bartering system; if I do this, God will do that. I'm either saved by works (what I do), emotions (what I experience), or knowledge (what I know).

By contrast, Christianity has no whiff of negotiation at all. Man is not the negotiator; indeed, man has no grounds from which to negotiate.

MAX LUCADO
IN THE GRIP OF GRACE

Imagine coming to a friend's house who has invited you over to enjoy a meal. You finish the delicious meal and then listen to some fine music and visit for a while. Finally, you stand up and get your coat as you prepare to leave. But before you leave you reach into your pocket and say, "Now, how much do I owe you?" What an insult! You don't do that with someone who has graciously given you a meal. Isn't it strange, though, how this world is running over with people who think there's something they must do to pay God back? Somehow they are hoping God will smile on them if they work real hard and earn his acceptance; but that's an acceptance on the basis of works. That's not the way it is with grace.

And now that Christ has come and died and thereby satisfied the Father's demands on sin, all we need to do is claim his grace by accepting the free gift of eternal life. Period.

HE SMILES ON
US BECAUSE OF
HIS SON'S DEATH
AND RESURRECTION.
IT'S GRACE, MY FRIEND,
AMAZING GRACE.

CHARLES SWINDOLL
THE GRACE AWAKENING

HERE IS NO WAY OUR LITTLE MINDS CAN COMPREHEND THE LOVE OF GOD. BUT THAT DIDN'T KEEP HIM FROM COMING. . . .

From the cradle in Bethlehem
to the cross in Jerusalem we've
pondered the love of our Father. What
can you say to that kind of emotion?
Upon learning that God would rather
die than live without you, how do you
react? How can you begin to explain
such passion?

MAX LUCADO
IN THE GRIP OF GRACE

AN UNFAILING *Friend*

od's Book is a veritable storehouse of promises— over seven thousand of them. Not empty hopes and dreams, not just nice-sounding, eloquently worded thoughts that make you feel warm all over, but promises. Verbal guarantees in writing, signed by the Creator himself, in which he declares he will do or will refrain from doing specific things.

(CONTINUED)

In a world of liars, cheats, deceivers, and con artists, isn't it a relief to know there is Someone you can trust? If he said it, you can count on it. Unlike the rhetoric of politicians who promise anybody anything they want to hear to get elected, what God says, God does.

CHARLES SWINDOLL
THE FINISHING TOUCH

GOD'S GIFT TO US
CAME WRAPPED IN
SWADDLING CLOTHES
LYING IN A MANGER.
TALK ABOUT DOING
THE UNEXPECTED FOR
THE UNDERSERVING!

CHARLES SWINDOLL

e worry. We worry about the IRS and the SAT and the FBI. We worry about education, recreation, and constipation. We worry that we won't have enough money, and when we have money we worry that we won't manage it well. We worry that the world will end before the parking meter expires. We worry what the dog thinks if he sees us step out of the shower. We worry that someday we'll learn that fat-free yogurt was fattening.

(CONTINUED)

Honestly, now. Did God save you so you would fret? Would he teach you to walk just to watch you fall? Would he be nailed to the cross for your sins and then disregard your prayers? Come on. Is Scripture teasing us when it reads, "He has put his angels in charge of you to watch over you wherever you go"? (Ps. 91:11).

I don't think so either.

MAX LUCADO
IN THE GRIP OF GRACE

A SMALL CATHEDRAL OUTSIDE BETHLEHEM MARKS THE SUPPOSED BIRTHPLACE OF JESUS. Behind a high altar in the church is a cave, a little cavern lit by silver lamps.

You can enter the main edifice and admire the ancient church. You can also enter the quiet cave where a star embedded in the floor recognizes the birth of the King. There is one stipulation, however. You have to stoop. The door is so low you can't go in standing up.

The same is true of the Christ. You can see the world standing tall, but to witness the Savior, you have to get down on your knees.

. . . to witness the Savior, you have to get down on your knees.

MAX LUCADO
THE APPLAUSE OF HEAVEN

piano sits in a room, gathering dust. It is full of the music of the masters, but in order for such strains to flow from it, fingers must strike the keys . . . trained fingers, representing endless hours of disciplined dedication. You do not have to practice. The piano neither requires it nor demands it. If, however, you want to draw beautiful music from the piano, that discipline is required. . . .

(CONTINUED)

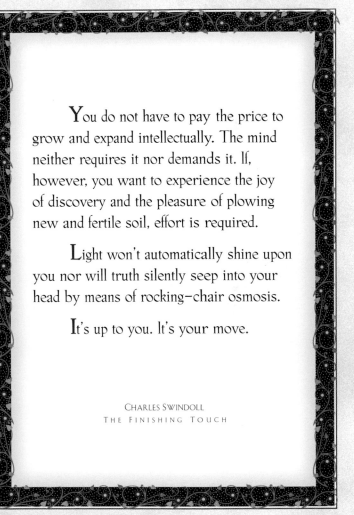

You do not have to pay the price to grow and expand intellectually. The mind neither requires it nor demands it. If, however, you want to experience the joy of discovery and the pleasure of plowing new and fertile soil, effort is required.

Light won't automatically shine upon you nor will truth silently seep into your head by means of rocking-chair osmosis.

It's up to you. It's your move.

CHARLES SWINDOLL
THE FINISHING TOUCH

YOU WANT TO MAKE A DIFFERENCE IN YOUR WORLD? LIVE A HOLY LIFE:

Be faithful to your spouse.

Be the one at the office who refuses to cheat.

Be the neighbor who acts neighborly.

Be the employee who does the work and doesn't complain.

Pay your bills.

Do your part and enjoy life.

Don't speak one message and live another.

PEOPLE ARE WATCHING
THE WAY WE ACT
MORE THAN THEY ARE
LISTENING TO
WHAT WE SAY.

Max Lucado
A Gentle Thunder

"God has planted eternity in the hearts of men."

Ecclesiastes 3:10 TLB

 HERE IS ONE WORD THAT DESCRIBES THE NIGHT HE CAME— ORDINARY.

The sky was ordinary. An occasional gust stirred the leaves and chilled the air. The stars were diamonds sparkling on black velvet. Fleets of clouds floated in front of the moon.

It was a beautiful night—a night worth peeking out your bedroom window to admire—but not really an unusual one. No reason to expect a surprise. Nothing to keep a person awake. An ordinary night with an ordinary sky.

(CONTINUED)

The sheep were ordinary. Some fat. Some scrawny. Some with barrel bellies. Some with twig legs. Common animals. No fleece made of gold. No history makers. No blue-ribbon winners. They were simply sheep—lumpy, sleeping silhouettes on a hillside.

And the shepherds. Peasants they were. Probably wearing all the clothes they owned. Smelling like sheep and looking just as woolly. They were conscientious, willing to spend the night with their flocks. But you won't find their staffs in a museum nor their writings in a library. No one asked their opinion on social justice or the application of the Torah. They were nameless and simple.

(CONTINUED)

An ordinary night with ordinary sheep and ordinary shepherds. And were it not for a God who loves to hook an "extra" on the front of the ordinary, the night would have gone unnoticed. The sheep would have been forgotten, and the shepherds would have slept the night away.

But God dances amidst the common. And that night he did a waltz.

(CONTINUED)

The black sky exploded with brightness. Trees that had been shadows jumped into clarity. Sheep that had been silent became a chorus of curiosity. One minute the shepherd was dead asleep, the next he was rubbing his eyes and staring into the face of an alien.

The night was ordinary no more.

The angel came in the night because that is when lights are best seen and that is when they are most needed. God comes into the common for the same reason.

HIS MOST POWERFUL TOOLS ARE THE SIMPLEST.

MAX LUCADO
THE APPLAUSE OF HEAVEN

Here is what we want to know. We want to know how long God's love will endure. . . . Does God really love us forever? Not just on Easter Sunday when our shoes are shined and our hair is fixed. We want to know . . . how does God feel about me when I'm a jerk? Not when I'm peppy and positive and ready to tackle world hunger. Not then. I know how he feels about me then. Even I like me then.

I want to know how he feels about me when I snap at anything that moves, when my thoughts are gutter-level, when my tongue is sharp enough to slice a rock. How does he feel about me then? . . .

(CONTINUED)

Can anything separate us from the love Christ has for us?

God answered our question before we asked it. So we'd see his answer, he lit the sky with a star. So we'd hear it, he filled the night with a choir; and so we'd believe it, he did what no man had ever dreamed. He became flesh and dwelt among us.

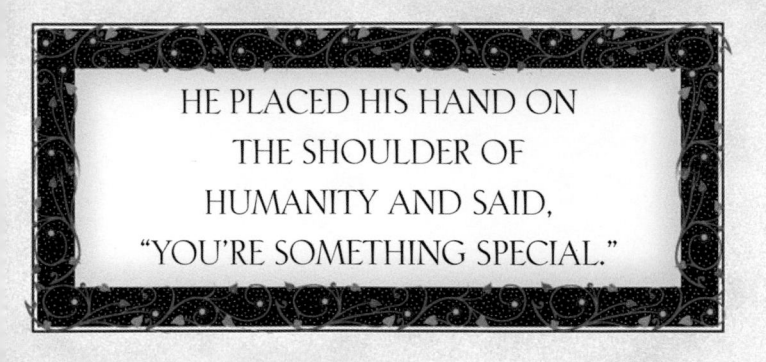

HE PLACED HIS HAND ON
THE SHOULDER OF
HUMANITY AND SAID,
"YOU'RE SOMETHING SPECIAL."

MAX LUCADO
IN THE GRIP OF GRACE

HE HEARS. HE SEES.
HE STAYS NEAR.
HE ACCEPTS US
AND LOVES US
UNCONDITIONALLY.
HE IS "THE FATHER OF
MERCIES AND THE GOD
OF ALL COMFORT."

CHARLES SWINDOLL
THE FINISHING TOUCH

rom a distance, we dazzle; up close, we're tarnished. Put enough of us together and we may resemble an impressive mountain range. But when you get down into the shadowy crevices . . . the Alps we ain't.

That's why our Lord means so much to us. He is intimately acquainted with all our ways. Darkness and light are alike to him. Not one of us is hidden from his sight.

(CONTINUED)

All things are open and laid
bare before him: our darkest secret,
our deepest shame, our stormy past, our
worst thought, our hidden motive, our
vilest imagination . . . even our
vain attempts to cover the ugly with
snow-white beauty.

He comes up so close. He sees
it all. He knows our frame. He remembers
we are dust.

BEST OF ALL, HE LOVES US STILL.

CHARLES SWINDOLL
THE FINISHING TOUCH

DISCIPLINE IS EASY
FOR ME TO SWALLOW.
LOGICAL TO ASSIMILAT
MANAGEABLE AND
APPROPRIATE.

But God's grace? Anything but.

Examples? How much time do you have?

David the psalmist becomes David the voyeur, but by God's grace becomes David the psalmist again.

Peter denied Christ before he preached Christ.

Zacchaeus, the crook. The cleanest part of his life was the money he'd laundered. But Jesus still had time for him. . . .

Story after story. Prayer after prayer. Surprise after surprise.

Seems that God is looking more for ways to get us home than for ways to keep us out. I challenge you to find one soul who came to God seeking grace and did not find it.

MAX LUCADO
WHEN GOD WHISPERS YOUR NAME

I t occurred to me last week that there is a practical reason Thanksgiving always precedes Christmas: It sets in motion the ideal mental attitude to carry us through the weeks in between. In other words, a sustained spirit of gratitude makes the weeks before Christmas a celebration rather than a marathon.

Maybe these few thoughts will stimulate you to give God your own thanks in greater abundance.

THANK YOU LORD;

for Your sovereign control over our circumstances
for Your holy character in spite of our sinfulness
for Your commitment to us even when we
    wander astray
for Your Word that gives us direction
for Your love that holds us close
for Your gentle compassion in our sorrows
for Your consistent faithfulness through our
    highs and lows . . .
for Your understanding when we are confused
for Your Spirit that enlightens our eyes
for Your grace that removes our guilt

CHARLES SWINDOLL   THE FINISHING TOUCH

CHRISTMAS STRIPS
AWAY THE VENEER OF
STACKED–UP YEARS
AND BRINGS US BACK
TO WHERE WE STARTED.

CHARLES SWINDOLL

ant to see a miracle? Plant a word of love heartdeep in a person's life. Nurture it with a smile and a prayer, and watch what happens.

An employee gets a compliment. A wife receives a bouquet of flowers. A cake is baked and carried next door. A widow is hugged. A gas-station attendant is honored. A preacher is praised.

(CONTINUED)

Sowing seeds of peace is like sowing beans. You don't know why it works; you just know it does. Seeds are planted, and topsoils of hurt are shoved away.

DON'T FORGET THE PRINCIPLE. NEVER UNDERESTIMATE THE POWER OF A SEED.

MAX LUCADO
THE APPLAUSE OF HEAVEN

ntethered by time, [God] sees us all. From the backwoods of Virginia to the business district of London; from the Vikings to the astronauts, from the cave-dwellers to the kings, from the hut-builders to the finger-pointers to the rock-stackers, he sees us. Vagabonds and ragamuffins all, he saw us before we were born.

And he loves what he sees. Flooded by emotion. Overcome by pride, the Starmaker turns to us, one by one, and says, "You are my child. I love you dearly. I'm aware that someday you'll turn from me and walk away. But I want you to know, I've already provided a way back."

And to prove it, he did something extraordinary.

(CONTINUED)

48

Stepping from the throne, he removed his robe of light and wrapped himself in skin: pigmented, human skin. The light of the universe entered a dark, wet womb. He whom angels worship nestled himself in the placenta of a peasant, was birthed into the cold night, and then slept on cow's hay.

Mary didn't know whether to give him milk or give him praise, but she gave him both since he was, as near as she could figure, hungry and holy.

Joseph didn't know whether to call him Junior or Father. But in the end called him Jesus, since that's what the angel had said and since he didn't have the faintest idea what to name a God he could cradle in his arms.

(CONTINUED)

. . . Don't you think . . . their heads tilted and their minds wondered, "What in the world are you doing, God?" Or, better phrased, "God, what are you doing in the world?"

"Can anything make me stop loving you?" God asks. "Watch me speak your language, sleep on your earth, and feel your hurts. Behold the maker of sight and sound as he sneezes, coughs, and blows his nose. You wonder if I understand how you feel? Look into the dancing eyes of the kid in Nazareth; that's God walking to school. Ponder the toddler at Mary's table; that's God spilling his milk.

(CONTINUED)

"You wonder how long my love will last? Find your answer on a splintered cross, on a craggy hill. That's me you see up there, your maker, your God, nail-stabbed and bleeding. Covered in spit and sin-soaked.

"THAT'S YOUR SIN I'M FEELING. THAT'S YOUR DEATH I'M DYING. THAT'S YOUR RESURRECTION I'M LIVING. THAT'S HOW MUCH I LOVE YOU."

MAX LUCADO
IN THE GRIP OF GRACE

When you give
yourself, the gift never
has to be returned.

Charles Swindoll

S *eren–dip–ity*—the *dip* of the *serene* into the common responsibilities of life. Serendipity occurs when something beautiful breaks into the monotonous and the mundane. A serendipitous life is marked by "surprisability" and spontaneity. When we lose our capacity for either, we settle into life's ruts. We expect little, and we're seldom disappointed.

Though I have walked with God for several decades, I must confess I still find much about him incomprehensible and mysterious. But this much I know: He delights in surprising us. He dots our pilgrimage from earth to heaven with amazing serendipities. . . .

Your situation may be as hot and barren as a desert or as forlorn and meaningless as a wasteland. You may be tempted to think, "There's no way!" when someone suggests things could change.

ALL I ASK IS THAT YOU . . .

BE ON THE LOOKOUT.

GOD MAY VERY WELL BE

PLANNING A SERENDIPITY

IN YOUR LIFE.

CHARLES SWINDOLL
THE FINISHING TOUCH

ECAUSE IT IS SHORT, LIFE IS PACKED WITH CHALLENGING POSSIBILITIES. Because it is uncertain, it's filled with challenging adjustments. I'm convinced that's much of what Jesus meant when he promised us an abundant life. Abundant with challenges, running over with possibilities, filled with opportunities to adapt, shift, alter, and change. Come to think of it, that's the secret of staying young. It is also the path that leads to optimism and motivation.

(CONTINUED)

With each new dawn, life delivers a package to your front door, rings your doorbell, and runs. Each package is cleverly wrapped in paper with big print. One package reads: "Watch out. Better worry about this!" Another: "Danger. This will bring fear!" And another: "Impossible. You'll never handle this one!"

When you hear that ring tomorrow morning, try something new. Have Jesus Christ answer the door for you.

CHARLES SWINDOLL
THE FINISHING TOUCH

57

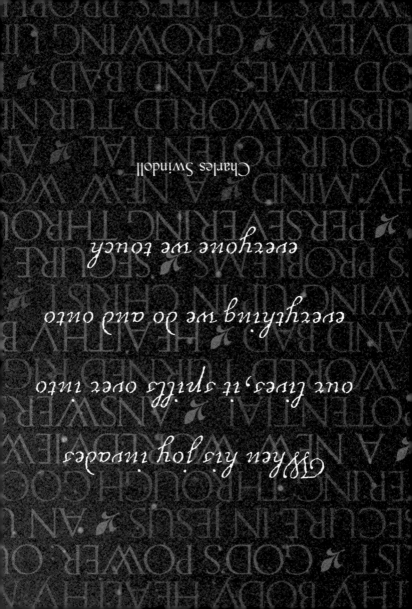

When his joy invades
our lives, it spills over into
everything we do and onto
everyone we touch

Charles Swindoll

GODLINESS IS
SOMETHING
BELOW THE
SURFACE OF
A LIFE, DEEP DOWN IN
THE REALM OF ATTITUDE . . .
AN ATTITUDE TOWARD
GOD HIMSELF.

The longer I think about this, the more I believe that a person who is godly is one whose heart is sensitive toward God, one who takes God seriously. This evidences itself in one very obvious mannerism: the godly individual hungers and thirsts after God. In the words of the psalmist, the godly person has a soul that "pants" for the living God (Ps. 42:1–2).

Godly people possess an attitude of willing submission to God's will and ways. Whatever he says goes. And whatever it takes to carry it out is the very thing the godly desire to do.

CHARLES SWINDOLL   THE FINISHING TOUCH

Somewhere, miles away, crops push their way toward harvest and waves roar and tumble onto shore. Windswept forests sing their timeless songs, and desert animals scurry in the shadows of cactus and rock.

Within a matter of hours night will fall, the dark sky will glitter with moon and stars, and sleep will force itself upon us. Life will continue on uninterrupted. Appreciated or not, the canvas of nature will go on being painted by the fingers of God.

In the midst of the offensive noise of our modern world—the people, the cars, the sounds, the smog, the heat, the pressures—there stand those reminders of his deep peace.

THE RUNNING WAVE, THE FLOWING
AIR, THE QUIET EARTH, THE SHINING
STARS, THE GENTLE NIGHT, THE
HEALING LIGHT . . . AND FROM EACH,
THE BLESSING OF THE DEEP PEACE OF
CHRIST TO YOU, TO ME.

CHARLES SWINDOLL
THE FINISHING TOUCH

Acknowledgments

Grateful acknowledgment is made to the following
publishers and copyright holders for permission
to reprint copyrighted material:

MAX LUCADO

* *The Applause of Heaven.* Dallas: Word. © Max Lucado, 1990, 1996.

* *When God Whispers Your Name.* Dallas: Word. © Max Lucado, 1994.

* *A Gentle Thunder.* Dallas: Word. © Max Lucado, 1995.

* *In the Grip of Grace.* Dallas: Word. © Max Lucado, 1996.

CHARLES SWINDOLL

* *The Grace Awakening.* Dallas: Word. © Charles Swindoll, 1990.

* *The Finishing Touch.* Dallas: Word. © Charles Swindoll, 1994.

* *Flying Closer to the Flame.* Dallas: Word. © Charles Swindoll, 1993, 1995